A Briefe and True Report of the New Found Land Of Virginia

Thomas Hariot

Contents

A BRIEFE AND TRUE REPORT OF THE NEW FOUND LAND OF VIRGINIA

by

Thomas Hariot

A Briefe and True Report ...
by Thomas Hariot

A briefe and true report
of the new found land of Virginia,
'of the commodities and of the nature and man
ners of the naturall inhabitants: Discouered by
the English Colony there seated by' Sir Richard
Greinuile Knight' 'In the yeere 1585. Which remained
vnder the gouernment of twelue monethes,
At the speciall charge and direction of the Honourable
rable' SIR WALTER RALEIGH Knight, 'lord Warden
of the stanneries Who therein hath beene fauoured
and authorised by her' MAIESTIE
':and her letters patents:
This fore booke Is made in English
By Thomas Hariot; seruant to the abouenamed
Sir' WALTER, 'a member of the Colony, and there
imployed in discouering.'

CVM GRATIA ET PRIVILEGIO CAES.MATIS SPECIALD

FRANCOFORTI AD MOENVM
TYPIS IOANNIS WECHELI, SVMTIBVS VERO THEODORI
DE BRY ANNO CD D XC.
VENALES REPERIVNTVR IN OFFICINA SIGISMVNDI FEIRABENDII

TO THE RIGHT
WORTHIE AND HONOVRABLE
SIR VVALTER RALEGH,
KNIGHT, SENESCHAL OF THE DVCHIES OF
Cornewall and Exeter, and L. Warden of the stannaries in Deuon
and Cornewall, T.B. wisheth true felicitie.

IR, seeing that the parte of the Worlde, which is betwene the FLORIDA
and the Cap BRETON nowe nammed VIRGINIA, to the honneur of yours
most souueraine Layde and Queene ELIZABETZ, hath ben descouuerd by
yours meanes. And great chardges. And that your Collonye hath been theer
established to your great honnor and prayse, and noelesser proffit vnto the common
welth: Yt ys good raison that euery man euertwe him selfe for to showe the benefit
which they haue receue of yt. Theerfore, for my parte I haue been allwayes Desir-
ous for to make yow knowe the good will that I haue to remayne still your most
humble saruant. I haue thincke that I cold faynde noe better occasion to declare yt,
then takinge the paines to cott in copper (the most diligent ye and well that wear in
my possible to doe) the Figures which doe leuelye represent the forme aud maner
of the Inhabitants of the sane countrye with theirs ceremonies, sollemne,, feastes,
and the manner and situation of their Townes of Villages. Addinge vnto euery fig-
ure a brief declaration of the same, to that ende that cuerye man cold the better
vnderstand that which is in liuely represented. Moreouer I haue thincke that the
aforesaid figures wear of greater commendation, If somme Histoire which traitinge
of the commodites and fertillitye of the rapport which Thomas Hariot hath lattely
sett foorth, and haue causse them booth togither to be printed for to dedicated vnto

you, as a thiuge which by reigtte dooth allreadye apparteyne vnto you. Therfore doe I creaue that you will accept this little Booke, and take yt In goode partte. And desiring that fauor that you will receue me in the nomber of one of your most humble seruantz, besechinge the lord to blese and further you in all yours good doinges and actions, and allso to preserue, and keepe you allwayes in good helthe. And so I comitt you unto the almyhttie, from Franckfort the first of Apprill 1590.'

'Your most humble seruant,'

THEODORVS de BRY.

TO THE ADVENTVRERS, FAVORERS,
AND VVELVVILLERS OF THE
ENTERPRISE FOR THE INHABITTING
and planting in VIRGINIA.

SINCE the first vndertaking by Sir Walter Ralegh to deale in the action of
discouering of that Countrey which is now called and known by the name
of VIRGINIA; many voyages hauing bin thiter made at sundrie times to his
great charge; as first in the yeere 1584. and afterwardes in the yeeres 1585.
'1586'. and now of late this last yeare of '1587'. There haue bin diuers and variable
reportes with some slaunderous and shamefull speeches bruited abroade by many
that returned from thence. Especially of that discouery which was made by the
Colony transported by Sir Richard Greinuile in the yeare '1585'. being of all the
others the most principal and as yet of most effect, the time of their abode in the
countrey beeing a whole yeare, when as in the other voyage before they staied but
six weekes; and the others after were onelie for supply and transportation, nothing more being discouered then had been before. Which reports haue not done a
litle wrong to many that otherwise would have also fauoured & aduentured in the
action, to the honour and benefite of our nation, besides the particular profite and
credite which would redound to them selues the dealers therein; as I hope by the
sequele of euents to the shame of those that haue auouched the contrary shalbe
manifest: if you the aduenturers, fauourers, and welwillers do but either encrease
in number, or in opinion continue, or hauing bin doubtfull renewe your good lik-
ing and furtherance to deale therein according to the worthinesse thereof alreadye
found and as you shall vnderstand hereafter to be requisite. Touching which woor-

thines through cause of the diuersitie of relations and reportes, manye of your opinions coulde not bee firme, nor the mindes of some that are well disposed, bee setled in any certaintie.

I haue therefore thought it good beeing one that haue beene in the discouerie and in dealing with the natuall inhabitantes specially imploied; and hauing therefore seene and knowne more then the ordinaire: to imparte so much vnto you of the fruites of our labours, as that you may knowe howe iniuriously the enterprise is slaundered. And that in publike manner at this present chiefelie for two respectes.

First that some of you which are yet ignorant or doubtfull of the state thereof, may see that there is sufficiet cause why the cheefe enterpriser with the fauour of her Maiestie, notwithstanding suche reportes; hath not onelie since continued the action by sending into the countrey againe, and replanting this last yeere a new Colony; but is also readie, according as the times and meanes will affoorde, to follow and prosecute the same.

Secondly, that you seeing and knowing the continuance of the action by the view hereof you may generally know & learne what the countrey is; & therevpon cosider how your dealing therein if it proceede, may returne you profit and gaine; bee it either by inhabitting & planting or otherwise in furthering thereof.

And least that the substance of my relation should be doubtful vnto you, as of others by reason of their diuersitie: I will first open the cause in a few wordes wherefore they are so different; referring my selue to your fauourable constructions, and to be adiudged of as by good consideration you shall finde cause.

Of our companie that returned some for their misdemenour and ill dealing in the countrey, haue beene there worthily punished; who by reason of their badde natures, haue maliciously not onelie spoken ill of their Gouernours; but for their sakes slaundered the countrie it selfe. The like also haue those done which were of their confort.

Some beeing ignorant of the state thereof, nothwithstanding since their returne amongest their friendes and acquaintance and also others, especially if they were in companie where they might not be gainesaide; woulde seeme to know so much as no men more; and make no men so great trauailers as themselues. They stood so much as it maie seeme vppon their credite and reputation that hauing been a twelue moneth in the countrey, it woulde haue beene a great disgrace vnto them as they thought, if they coulde not haue saide much wheter it were true or false. Of which some haue spoken of more then euer they saw or otherwise knew to bee there; othersome haue not bin ashamed to make absolute deniall of that which although not by the, yet by others is most certainely ad there pletifully knowne. And othersome make difficulties of those things they haue no skill of.

The cause of their ignorance was, in that they were of that many that were neuer out of the Iland where wee were seated, or not farre, or at the leastwise in few places els, during the time of our aboade in the countrey; or of that many that after golde and siluer was not so soone found, as it was by them looked for, had little or no care of any other thing but to pamper their bellies; or of that many which had little vnderstanding, lesse discretion, and more tongue then was needfull or requisite.

Some also were of a nice bringing vp, only in cities or townes, or such as neuer (as I may say) had seene the world before. Because there were not to bee found any English cities, norsuch faire houses, nor at their owne wish any of their olde accustomed daintie food, nor any soft beds of downe or fethers: the countrey was to them miserable, & their reports thereof according.

Because my purpose was but in briefe to open the cause of the varietie of such speeches; the particularities of them, and of many enuious, malicious, and slauderous reports and deuises els, by our owne countrey men besides; as trifles that are not worthy of wise men to bee thought vpon, I meane not to trouble you withall: but will passe to the commodities, the substance of that which I haue to make relation of vnto you.

The treatise where of for your more readie view & easier vnderstanding I will diuide into three speciall parts. In the first I will make declaration of such commodities there alreadie found or to be raised, which will not onely serue the ordinary turnes of you which are and shall bee the platers and inhabitants, but such an ouerplus sufficiently to bee yelded, or by men of skill to bee prouided, as by way of trafficke and exchaunge with our owne nation of England, will enrich your selues the prouiders; those that shal deal with you; the enterprisers in general; and greatly profit our owne countrey men, to supply them with most things which heretofore they haue bene faine to prouide, either of strangers or of our enemies: which commodities for distinction sake, I call 'Merchantable'.

In the second, I will set downe all the comodities which wee know the countrey by our experience doeth yeld of its selfe for victuall, and sustenance of mans life; such as is vsually fed vpon by the inhabitants of the countrey, as also by vs during the time we were there.

In the last part I will make mention generally of such other comodities besides, as I am able to remember, and as I shall thinke behoofull for those that shall inhabite, and plant there to knowe of; which specially concerne building, as also some other necessary vses: with a briefe description of the nature and maners of the people of the countrey.

THE FIRST PART,
OF MARCHANTABLE COMMODITIES.

'Silke of grasse or grasse Silke.'

THere is a kind of grasse in the countrey vppon the blades where of there groweth very good silke in forme of a thin glittering skin to bee stript of. It groweth two foote and a halfe high or better: the blades are about two foot in length, and half inch broad. The like groweth in Persia, which is in the selfe same climate as Virginia, of which very many of the silke workes that come from thence into Europe are made. Here of if it be planted and ordered as in Persia, it cannot in reason be otherwise, but that there will rise in shorte time great profite to the dealers therein; seeing there is so great vse and vent thereof as well in our countrey as els where. And by the meanes of sowing & plating in good ground, it will be farre greater, better, and more plentifull then it is. Although notwithstanding there is great store thereof in many places of the countrey growing naturally and wilde. Which also by proof here in England, in making a piece of silke Grogran, we found to be excellent good.

'Worme Silke.'

In manie of our iourneyes we found silke wormes fayre and great; as bigge as our ordinary walnuttes. Although it hath not beene our happe to haue found such plentie as elsew here to be in the coutrey we haue heard of; yet seeing that the countrey doth naturally breede and nourish them, there is no doubt but if art be added in plantig of mulbery trees and others fitte for them in commodious places, for their feeding and nourishing; and some of them carefully gathered and husbanded in that sort as by men of skill is knowne to be necessarie: there will rise as great profite in time to the Virginians, as there of doth now to the Persians, Turkes, Italians, and Spaniards.

'Flaxe and Hempe.'

The trueth is that of Hempe and Flaxe there is no greate store in any one place together, by reason it is not planted but as the soile doth yeeld it of it selfe; and howsoeuer the leafe, and stemme or stalke doe differ from ours; the stuffe by the iudgemet of men of skill is altogether as good as ours. And if not, as further proofe should finde otherwise; we haue that experience of the soile, as thas there canno bee shewed anie reason to the contrary, but that it will grow there excellent well; and by planting will be yeelded plentifully: seeing there is so much ground whereof some may well be applyed to such purposes. What benefite heereof may growe in cordage and linnens who can not easily vnderstand?

'Allum.'

There is a veine of earth along the sea coast for the space of fourtie or fiftie miles, whereof by the iudgement of some that have made triall heere in England, is made good Allum, of that kinde which is called Roche Allum. The richnesse of such a commoditie is so well knowne that I neede not to saye any thing thereof. The same earth doth also yeelde White Copresse, Nitrum, and Alumen Plumeum, but nothing so plentifully as the common Allum; which be also of price and profitable.

'Wapeih:'

Wapeih, a kinde of earth so called by the naturall inhabitants; very like to terra sigillata: and hauing beene refined, it hath beene found by some of our Phisitios and Chirurgeons to bee of the same kinde of vertue and more effectuall. The inhabitats vfe it very much for the cure of sores and woundes: there is in diuers places great plentie, and in some places of a blewe sort.

'Pitch, Tarre, Rozen, and Turpentine.'

There are those kindes of trees which yeelde them abundantly and great store. In the very same Iland where wee were seated, being fifteene miles of length, and fiue or six miles in breadth, there are fewe trees els but of the same kind; the whole Iland being full.

'Sassafras.'

Sassafras, called by the inhabitantes Winauk, a kinde of wood of most pleasand and sweete smel; and of most rare vertues in phisick for the cure of many diseases. It is found by experience to bee farre better and of more vses then the wood which is called Guaiacum, or Lignum vita. For the description, the manner of vsing and the manifolde vertues thereof, I referre you to the booke of Monardus, translated and entituled in English, The ioyfull newes from the West Indies.

'Cedar.'

Cedar, a very sweet wood & fine timber; whereof if nests of chests be there made, or timber therof fitted for sweet & fine bedsteads, tables, or deskes, lutes, virginalles & many things else, (of which there hath beene proofe made already) to make vp fraite with other principal commodities will yeeld profite.

'Wine.'

There are two kinds of grapes that the soile doth yeeld naturally: the one is small and sowre of the ordinarie bignesse as ours in England: the other farre greater & of himselfe iushious sweet. When they are plated and husbandeg as they ought, a principall commoditie of wines by them may be raised.

'Oyle.'

There are two sortes of Walnuttes both holding oyle, but the one farre more plentifull then the other. When there are milles & other deuises for the purpose, a commodity of them may be raised because there are infinite store. There are also three seuerall kindes of Berries in the forme of Oke akornes, which also by the experience and vse of the inhabitantes, wee finde to yeelde very good and sweete oyle. Furthermore the Beares of the countrey are commonly very fatte, and in some places there are many: their fatnesse because it is so liquid, may well be termed oyle, and hath many speciall vses.

'Furres:'

All along the Sea coast there are great store of Otters, which beeying taken by weares and other engines made for the purpose, will yeelde good profite. Wee hope also of Marterne furres, and make no doubt by the relation of the people but that in some places of the countrey there are store: although there were but two skinnes that came to our handes. Luzarnes also we haue vnderstading of. although for the time we saw none.

'Deare skinnes.'

Deare skinnes dressed after the manner of Chamoes or vndressed are to be had of the naturall inhabitants thousands yeerely by way of trifficke for trifles: and no more wast or spoile of Deare then is and hath beene ordinarily in time before.

'Ciuet cattes.'

In our trauailes, there was founde one to haue beene killed by a saluage or inhabitant: and in an other place the smell where one or more had lately beene before: whereby we gather besides then by the relation of the people that there are some in the countrey: good profite will rise by them.

'Iron.'

In two places of the countrey specially, one about fourescore and the other sixe score miles from the Fort or place where wee dwelt: wee founde neere the water side the ground to be rockie, which by the triall of a minerall man, was founde to holde Iron richly. It is founde in manie places of the countrey else. I knowe nothing to the contrarie, but that it maie bee allowed for a good marchantable commoditie, considering there the small charge for the labour and feeding of men: the infinite store of wood: the want of wood and deerenesse thereof in England: & the necessity of ballasting of shippes.

'Copper.'

A hundred and fiftie miles into the maine in two townes wee founde with the inhabitaunts diuerse small plates of copper, that had beene made as wee vnderstood, by the inhabitantes that dwell farther into the countrey: where as they say are mountaines and Riuers that yeelde also whyte graynes of Mettall, which is to bee deemed Siluer. For confirmation whereof at the time of our first arriuall in the Countrey, I sawe with some others with mee, two small peeces of siluer grosly beaten about the weight of a Testrone, hangyng in the eares of a Wiroans or chiefe Lorde that dwelt about fourescore myles from vs; of whom thorowe enquiry, by the number of dayes and the way, I learned that it had come to his handes from the same place or neere, where I after vnderstood the copper was made and the white graynes of mettall founde. The aforesaide copper wee also founde by triall to holde siluer.

'Pearle.'

Sometimes in feeding on muscles wee founde some pearle; but it was our hap to meete with ragges, or of a pide colour; not hauing yet discouered those places where wee hearde of better and more plentie. One of our companie; a man of skill in such matters, had gathered to gether from among the sauage people aboute fiue thousande: of which number he chose so many as made a fayre chaine, which for their likenesse and vniformitie in roundnesse, orientnesse, and pidenesse of may excellent colours, with equalitie in greatnesse, were verie fayer and rare; and had therefore beene presented to her Maiestie, had wee not by casualtie and through extremity of a storme, lost them with many things els in comming away from the countrey.

'Sweete Gummes.'

Sweete Gummes of diuers kindes and many other Apothecary drugges of which wee will make speciall mention, when wee shall receiue it from such men of skill in that kynd, that in taking reasonable paines shall discouer them more particularly then wee haue done; and than now I can makc relation of, for want of the examples I had prouited and gathered, and are nowe lost. with other thinges by causualtie before mentioned.

'Dyes of diuers kindes.'

There is Shoemake well knowen, and vsed in England for blacke; the seede of an hearbe called Wasewowr; little small rootes called Chappacor; and the barke of the tree called by the inhabitaunts Tangomockonomindge: which Dies are for diuers sortes of red: their goodnesse for our English clothes remayne yet to be proued. The inhabitants vse them onely for the dying of hayre; and colouring of their faces, aud Mantles made of Deare skinnes; and also for the dying of Rushes to make artificiall workes withall in their Mattes and Baskettes; hauing no other thing besides that they account of, apt to vse them for. If they will not proue merchantable there is no doubt but the Planters there shall finde apte vses for them, as also for other colours which wee knowe to be there.

'Oade.'

A thing of so great vent and vse amongst English Diers, which cannot bee yeelded sufficiently in our owne countrey for spare of ground; may bee planted in Virginia, there being ground enough. The grouth therof need not to be doubted when as in the Ilandes of the Asores it groweth plentifully, which is in thesame climate. So likewise of Madder.

'Suger canes.'

Whe carried thither Suger canes to plant which beeing not so well preserued as was requisit, & besides the time of the yere being past for their setting when we arriued, wee could not make that proofe of them as wee desired. Notwithstading, seeing that they grow in the same climate, in the South part of Spaine and in Barbary, our hope in reason may yet continue. So likewise for Orenges, and Lemmons, there may be planted also Quinses. Wherebi may grow in reasonable time if the action be diligently prosecuted, no small commodities in Sugers, Suckets, and Marmalades.

Many other commodities by planting may there also bee raised, which I leaue to your discret and gentle considerations: and many also may bee there which yet we haue not discouered. Two more commodities of great value one of certaintie, and the other in hope, not to be planted, but there to be raised & in short time to be prouided and prepared, I might have specified. So likewise of those commodities already set downe I might haue said more; as of the particular places where they are founde and best to be planted and prepared: by what meanes and in what reasonable space of time they might be raised to profit and in what proportion; but because others then welwillers might bee therewithall acquainted, not to the good of the action, I haue wittingly omitted them: knowing that to those that are well disposed I haue vttered, according to my promise and purpose, for this part sufficient.

THE SECOND PART,
OF SVCHE COMMODITIES AS VIRGINIA IS

knowne to yeelde for victuall and sustenace of mans
life, vsually fed vpon by the naturall inhabitants:
as also by vs during the time of our aboad.
And first of such as are sowed
and husbanded.

PAGATOWR, a kinde of graine so called by the inhabitants; the same in the West Indies is called MAYZE: English men call it Guinney wheate or Turkie wheate, according to the names of the countreys from whence the like hath beene brought. The graine is about the bignesse of our ordinary English peaze and not much different in forme and shape: but of diuers colours: some white, some red, some yellow, and some blew. All of them yeelde a very white and sweete flowre: beeing vsed according to his kinde it maketh a very good bread. Wee made of the same in the countrey some mault, whereof was brued as good ale as was to bee desired. So likewise by the help of hops therof may bee made as good Beere. It is a graine of marueilous great increase; of a thousand, fifteene hundred and some two thousand fold. There are three sortes, of which two are ripe in an eleuen and twelue weekes at the most: sometimes in ten, after the time they are set, and are then of height in stalke about six or seuen foote. The other sort is ripe in fourteene, and is about ten foote high, of the stalkes some beare foure heads, some three, some one, and two: euery head cotaining fiue, sixe, or seue hundred graines within a fewe more or lesse. Of these graines besides bread, the inhabitants make victuall eyther by parching them; or seething them whole vntill they be broken; or boyling the floure with water into a pappe.

'Okindgier', called by vs 'Beanes', because in greatnesse & partly in shape they are like to the Beanes in England; sauing that they are flatter, of more diuers colours, and some pide. The leafe also of the stemme is much different. In taste they are altogether as good as our English peaze.

'Wickonzowr', called by vs 'Peaze', in respect of the beanes for distinction sake, because they are much lesse; although in forme they little differ; but in goodnesse of tast much, & are far better then our English peaze. Both the beanes and peaze are ripe in tenne weekes after they are set. They make them victuall either by boyling them all to pieces into a broth; or boiling them whole vntill they bee soft and beginne to breake as is vsed in England, eyther by themselues or mixtly together: Sometime they mingle of the wheate with them. Sometime also beeing whole soddeu, they bruse or pound them in a morter, & thereof make loaues or lumps of dowishe bread, which they vse to eat for varietie.

'Macocqwer', according to their seuerall formes called by vs, 'Pompions', 'Mellions', and 'Gourdes', because they are of the like formes as those kindes in England. In 'Virginia' such of seuerall formes are of one taste and very good, and do also spring from one seed. There are of two sorts; one is ripe in the space of a moneth, and the other in two moneths.

There is an hearbe which in Dutch is called 'Melden'. Some of those that I

describe it vnto, take it to be a kinde of Orage; it groweth about foure or fiue foote
high: of the seede thereof they make a thicke broth, and pottage of a very good taste:
of the stalke by burning into ashes they make a kinde of salt earth, wherewithall
many vse sometimes to season their brothes; other salte they knowe not. Wee our
selues, vsed the leaues also for pothearbes.

There is also another great hearbe in forme of a Marigolde, about sixe foote in
height; the head with the floure is a spanne in breadth. Some take it to bee 'Planta
Solis': of the seedes heereof they make both a kinde of bread and broth.

All the aforesaid commodities for victuall are set or sowed, sometimes in
groundes a part and seuerally by themselues; but for the most part together in one
ground mixtly: the manner thereof with the dressing and preparing of the groud,
because I will note vnto you the fertilitie of the soile; I thinke good briefly to describe.

The ground they neuer fatten with mucke, dounge or any other thing; neither
plow nor digge it as we in England, but onely prepare it in sort as followeth. A fewe
daies before they sowe or set, the men with wooden instruments, made almost
in forme of mattockes or hoes with long handles; the women with short peckers
or parers, because they vse them sitting, of a foote long and about fiue inches in
breadth: doe onely breake the vpper part of the ground to rayse vp the weedes,
grasse, & old stubbes of corne stalkes with their rootes. The which after a day or
twoes drying in the Sunne, being scrapte vp into many small heapes, to saue them
labour for carrying them away; they burne into ashes. (And whereas some may
thinke that they vse the ashes for to better the grounde; I say that then they woulde
eyther disperse the ashes abroade; which wee obserued they doe not, except the
heapes bee too great: or els would take speciall care to set their corne where the
ashes lie, which also wee finde they are carelesse of.) And this is all the husbanding
of their ground that they vse.

Then their setting or sowing is after this maner. First for their corne, beginning in one corner of the plot, with a pecker they make a hole, wherein they put
foure graines with that care they touch not one another, (about an inch asunder)
and couer them with the moulde againe: and so through out the whole plot, making such holes and vsing them after such maner: but with this regard that they bee
made in rakes, euery ranke differing from other halfe a fadome or a yarde, and the

holes also in euery ranke, as much. By this meanes there is a yarde spare ground betwene euery hole: where according to discretion here and there, they set as many Beanes and Peaze: in diuers places also among the seedes of 'Macocqwer', 'Melden' and 'Planta Solis'.

The ground being thus set according to the rate by vs experimented, an English Acre conteining fourtie pearches in length, and foure in breadth, doeth there yeeld in croppe or ofcome of corne, beanes, and peaze, at the least two hudred London bushelles: besides the 'Macocqwer, Melden', and 'Planta Solis': When as in England fourtie bushelles of our wheate yeelded out of such an acre is thought to be much.

I thought also good to note this vnto you, if you which shall inhabite and plant there, maie know how specially that countrey corne is there to be preferred before ours: Besides the manifold waies in applying it to victuall, the increase is so much that small labour and paines is needful in respect that must be vsed for ours. For this I can assure you that according to the rate we haue made proofe of, one man may prepare and husbane so much grounde (hauing once borne corne before) with lesse the foure and twentie houres labour, as shall yeelde him victuall in a large proportio for a twelue moeth, if hee haue nothing else, but that which the same groud will yeelde, and of that kinde onelie which I haue before spoken of: the saide groud being also but of fiue and twentie yards square. And if neede require, but that there is ground enough, there might be raised out of one and the selfsame ground two haruestes or ofcomes; for they sowe or set and may at anie time when they thinke good from the middest of March vntill the ende of Iune: so that they also set when they haue eaten of their first croppe. In some places of the countrey notwithstanding they haue two haruests, as we haue heard, out of one and the same ground.

For English corne neuertheles whether to vse or not to vse it, you that inhabite maie do as you shall haue farther cause to thinke best. Of the grouth you need not to doubt: for barlie, oates and peaze, we haue seene proof of, not beeing purposely sowen but fallen casually in the worst sort of ground, and yet to be as faire as any we haue euer seene here in England. But of wheat because it was musty and hat taken salt water wee could make no triall: and of rye we had none. Thus much haue I digressed and I hope not vnnecessarily: nowe will I returne againe to my course and intreate of that which yet remaineth appertaining to this Chapter.

There is an herbe which is sowed a part by it selfe & is called by the inhabitants

Vppowoc: In the West Indies it hath diuers names, according to the seuerall places & countries where it groweth and is vsed: The Spaniardes generally call it Tobacco. The leaues thereof being dried and brought into powder: they vse to take the fume or smoke thereof by sucking it through pipes made of claie into their stomacke and heade; from whence it purgeth superfluous fleame & other grosse humors, openeth all the pores & passages of the body: by which meanes the vse thereof, not only pre-serueth the body from obstructios; but also if any be, so that they haue not beene of too long continuance, in short time breaketh them: wherby their bodies are notably preserued in health, & know not many greeuous diseases wherewithall wee in Eng-land are oftentimes afflicted.

The Vppowoc us of so precious estimation amongest then, that they thinke their gods are maruelously delighted therwith: Wherupon sometime they make hallowed fires & cast some of the pouder therein for a sacrifice: being in a storme vppon the waters, to pacifie their gods, they cast some vp into the aire and into the water: so a weare for fish being newly set vp, they cast some therein and into the aire: also after an escape of danger, they cast some into the aire likewise: but all done with strange gestures, stamping, somtime dauncing, clapping of hands, hold-ing vp of hands, & staring vp into rhe heauens, vttering therewithal and chattering strange words & noises.

We ourselues during the time we were there vsed to suck it after their maner, as also since our returne, & haue found manie rare and wonderful experiments of the vertues thereof; of which the relation woulde require a volume by it selfe: the vse of it by so manie of late, men & women of great calling as else, and some learned Phisitions also, is sufficient witnes.

And these are all the commodities for sustenance of life that I know and can remember they vse to husband: all else that followe are founde growing naturally or wilde.

'Of Rootes.'

OPENAVK are a kind of roots of round forme, some of the bignes of walnuts, some far greater, which are found in moist & marish grounds growing many to-gether one by another in ropes, or as thogh they were fastnened with a string. Being boiled or sodden they are very good meate.

OKEEPENAVK are also of round shape, found in dry grounds: some are of the bignes of a mans head. They are to be eaten as they are taken out of the ground, for by reason of their drinesse they will neither roste nor seeth. Their tast is not so good as of the former rootes, notwithstanding for want of bread & somtimes for varietie the inhabitants vse to eate them with fish or flesh, and in my iudgement they doe as well as the houshold bread made of rie heere in England.

'Kaishucpenauk' a white kind of roots about the bignes of hen egs & nere of that forme: their tast was not so good to our seeming as of the other, and therfore their place and manner of growing not so much cared for by vs: the inhabitats notwithstanding vsed to boile & eate many.

'Tsinaw' a kind of roote much like vnto the which in England is called the 'China root' brought from the East Indies. And we know not anie thing to the cotrary but that it maie be of the same kind. These roots grow manie together in great clusters and doe bring foorth a brier stalke, but the leafe in shape far vnlike; which beeing supported by the trees it groweth neerest vnto, wil reach or climbe to the top of the highest. From these roots while they be new or fresh beeing chopt into small pieces & stampt, is strained with water a iuice that maketh bread, & also being boiled, a very good spoonemeate in maner of a gelly, and is much better in tast if it bee tempered with oyle. This 'Tsinaw' is not of that sort which by some was caused to be brought into England for the 'China roote', for it was discouered since, and is in vfe as is aforesaide: but that which was brought hither is not yet knowne neither by vs nor by the inhabitants to serue for any vse or purpose; although the rootes in shape are very like.

'Coscushaw', some of our company tooke to bee that kinde of roote which the Spaniards in the West Indies call 'Cassauy', whereupon also many called it by that name: it groweth in very muddie pooles and moist groundes. Being dressed according to the countrey maner, it maketh a good bread, and also a good sponemeate, and is vsed very much by the inhabitants: The iuice of this root is poison, and therefore heede must be taken before any thing be made therewithal: Either the rootes must bee first sliced and dried in the Sunne, or by the fire, and then being pounded into floure wil make good bread: or els while they are greene they are to bee pared, cut into pieces and stampt; loues of the same to be laid neere or ouer the fire vntill it be soure, and then being well pounded againe, bread, or sponemeate very good in taste, and holsome may be made thereof.

'Habascon' is a roote of hoat taste almost of the forme and bignesse of a Pars-eneepe, of it selfe it is no victuall, but onely a helpe beeing boiled together with other meates.

There are also 'Leekes' differeing little from ours in England that grow in many places of the countrey, of which, when we came in places where, wee gathered and eate many, but the naturall inhabitants neuer.

'Of Fruites.'

CHESTNVTS, there are in diuers places great store: some they vse to eate rawe, some they stampe and boile to make spoonemeate, and with some being sodden they make such a manner of dowebread as they vfe of their beanes before mentioned.

WALNVTS: There are two kindes of Walnuts, and of then infinit store: In many places where very great woods for many miles together the third part of trees are walnuttrees. The one kind is of the same taste and forme or litle differing from ours of England, but that they are harder and thicker shelled: the other is greater and hath a verie ragged and harde shell: but the kernell great, verie oylie and sweete. Besides their eating of them after our ordinarie maner, they breake them with stones and pound them in morters with water to make a milk which they vse to put into some sorts of their spoonmeate; also among their sodde wheat, peaze, beanes and pompions which maketh them haue a farre more pleasant taste.

MEDLARS a kind of verie good fruit, so called by vs chieflie for these respectes: first in that they are not good vntill they be rotten: then in that they open at the head as our medlars, and are about the same bignesse: otherwise in taste and colour they are farre differet: for they are as red as cheries and very sweet: but whereas the cherie is sharpe sweet, they are lushious sweet.

METAQVESVNNAVK, a kinde of pleasaunt fruite almost of the shape & bignes of English peares, but that they are of a perfect red colour as well within as without. They grow on a plant whose leaues are verie thicke and full of prickles as sharpe as needles. Some that haue bin in the Indies, where they haue seen that kind of red die of great price which is called Cochinile to grow, doe describe his plant right like vnto this of Metaquesunnauk but whether it be the true Cochinile or a bastard or wilde kind, it cannot yet be certified; seeing that also as I heard, Cochinile is not of the fruite but founde on the leaues of the plant; which leaues for such matter we haue not so specially obserued.

GRAPES there are of two sorts which I mentioned in the marchantable comodities.

STRABERIES there are as good & as great as those which we haue in our English gardens.

MVLBERIES, Applecrabs, Hurts or Hurtleberies, such as wee haue in England.

SACQVENVMMENER a kinde of berries almost like vnto capres but some-
what greater which grow together in clusters vpon a plant or herb that is found in
shalow waters: being boiled eight or nine hours according to their kind are very
good meate and holesome, otherwise if they be eaten they will make a man for the
time franticke or extremely sicke.

There is a kind of reed which beareth a seed almost like vnto our rie or wheat,
& being boiled is good meate.

In our trauailes in some places wee founde wilde peaze like vnto ours in England but that they were lesse, which are also good meate.

'Of a kinde of fruite or berrie in the forme of Acornes.'

There is a kind of berrie or acorne, of which there are fiue sorts that grow on
seuerall kinds of trees; the one is called 'Sagatemener', the second 'Osamener', the
third 'Pummuckoner'. These kind of acorns they vse to drie vpon hurdles made of
reeds with fire vnderneath almost after the maner as we dry malt in England. When
they are to be vsed they first water them vntil they be soft & then being sod they
make a good victuall, either to eate so simply, or els being also pounded, to make
loaues or lumpes of bread. These be also the three kinds of which, I said before, the
inhabitants vsed to make sweet oyle.

An other sort is called 'Sapummener' which being boiled or parched doth eate
and taste like vnto chestnuts. They sometime also make bread of this sort.

The fifth sort is called 'Mangummenauk', and is the acorne of their kind of
oake, the which beeing dried after the maner of the first sortes, and afterward wa-
tered they boile them, & their seruants or sometime the chiefe theselues, either for
variety or for want of bread, doe eate them with their fish or flesh.

'Of Beastes.'

'Deare', in some places there are great store: neere vnto the sea coast they are of the ordinarie bignes as ours in England, & some lesse: but further vp into the countrey where there is better feed they are greater: they differ from ours onely in this, their tailes are longer and the snags of their hornes looke backward.

'Conies', Those that we haue seen & al that we can heare of are of a grey colour like vnto hares: in some places there are such plentie that all the people of some townes make them mantles of the furre or flue of the skinnes of those they vsually take.

'Saquenuckot' & 'Maquowoc'; two kindes of small beastes greater then conies which are very good meat. We neuer tooke any of them our selues, but sometime eate of such as the inhabitants had taken & brought vnto vs.

'Squirels' which are of a grey colour, we haue taken & eaten.

'Beares' which are all of black colour. The beares of this countrey are good meat; the inhabitants in time of winter do use to take & eate maie; so also somtime did wee. They are taken comonlie in this sort. In some Ilands or places where they are, being hunted for, as soone as they haue spiall of a man they presently run awaie, & then being chased they clime and get vp the next tree they can, from whence with arrowes they are shot downe starke dead, or with those wounds that they may after easily bekilled; we sometime shotte them downe with our caleeuers.

I haue the names of eight & twenty seuerall sortes of beasts which I haue heard of to be here and there dispersed in the countrie, especially in the maine: of which there are only twelue kinds that we haue yet discouered, & of those that be good meat we know only them before mentioned. The inhabitats somtime kil the 'Lyon' & eat him: & we somtime as they came to our hands of their 'Wolues' or 'woluish Dogges', which I haue not set downe for good meat, least that some woulde vnderstand my iudgement therin to be more simple than needeth, although I could alleage the difference in taste of those kindes from ours, which by some of our company haue been experimented in both.

'Of Foule.'

'Turkie cockes' and 'Turkie hennes': 'Stockdoues': 'Partridges': 'Cranes': 'Hernes': & in winter great store of 'Swannes' & 'Geese'. Of al sortes of foule I haue the names in the countrie language of fourescore and six of which number besides those that be named, we haue taken, eaten, & haue the pictures as they were there drawne with the names of the inhabitaunts of seuerall strange sortes of water foule eight, and seuenteene kindes more of land foul, although wee haue seen and eaten of many more, which for want of leasure there for the purpose coulde not bee pictured: and after wee are better furnished and stored vpon further discouery, with their strange beastes, fishe, trees, plants, and hearbes, they shall bee also published.

There are also 'Parats', 'Faulcons', & 'Marlin haukes', which although with vs they bee not vsed for meate, yet for other causes I thought good to mention.

'Of Fishe.'

For foure monthes of the yeere, February, March, Aprill and May, there are plentie of 'Sturgeons': And also in the same monethes of 'Herrings', some of the ordinary bignesse as ours in England, but the most part farre greater, of eighteene, twentie inches, and some two foote in length and better; both these kindes of fishe in those monethes are most plentifull, and in best season, which wee founde to bee most delicate and pleasaunt meate.

There are also 'Troutes, Porpoises, Rayes, Oldwiues, Mullets, Plaice,' and very many other sortes of excellent good fish, which we haue taken & eaten, whose names I know not but in the countrey language; wee haue of twelue sorts more the pictures as they were drawn in the countrey with their names.

The inhabitants vse to take then two maner of wayes, the one is by a kind of wear made of reedes which in that countrey are very strong. The other way which is more strange, is with poles make sharpe at one end, by shooting them into the fish after the maner as Irishmen cast dartes; either as they are rowing in their boates or els as they are wading in the shallowes for the purpose.

There are also in many places plentie of these kindes which follow.

'Sea crabbes', such as we haue in England.

'Oystres', some very great, and some small; some rounde and some of a long shape: They are founde both in salt water and brackish, and those that we had out of salt water are far better than the other as in our owne countrey.

Also 'Muscles, Scalopes, Periwinkles,' and 'Creuises'.

Seekanauk, a kind of crustie shell fishe which is good meate, about a foote in breadth, hauing a crustie tayle, many legges like a crab; and her eyes in her backe. They are founde in shallowes of salt waters; and sometime on the shoare.

There are many 'Tortoyses' both of lande and sea kinde, their backes & bellies are shelled very thicke; their head, feete, and taile, which are in appearance, seeme ougly as though they were members of a serpent or venemous: but notwithstanding they are very good meate, as also their egges. Some haue bene founde of a yard in bredth and better.

And thus haue I made relation of all sortes of victuall that we fed vpon for the time we were in 'Virginia', as also the inhabitants themselues, as farre foorth as I knowe and can remember or that are specially worthy to bee remembred.

THE THIRD AND LAST PART

OF SVCH OTHER
THINGES AS IS BE HOO-
full for those which shall plant and inhabit to
know of; with a description of the nature
and manners of the people of
the countrey.

'Of commodities for building and other
necessary uses.'

THose other things which I am more to make rehearsall of, are such as concerne building, and other mechanicall necessarie vses; as diuers sortes of trees for house & ship timber, and other vses els: Also lime, stone, and brick, least that being not mentioned some might haue bene doubted of, or by some that are malicious reported the contrary.

'Okes', there are as faire, straight, tall, and as good timber as any can be, and also great store, and in some places very great.

'Walnut trees', as I haue saide before very many, some haue bene seen excellent faire timber of foure & fiue fadome, & aboue fourescore foot streight without bough.

'Firre trees' fit for masts of ships, some very tall & great.

'Rakiock', a kind of trees so called that are sweet wood of which the inhabitans that were neere vnto vs doe commonly make their boats or Canoes of the form of trowes; only with the helpe of fire, harchets of stones, and shels; we haue known some so great being made in that sort of one tree that they haue carried well xx. men at once, besides much baggage: the timber being great, tal, streight, soft, light, & yet tough enough I thinke (besides other vses) to be fit also for masts of ships.

'Cedar', a sweet wood good for seelings, Chests, Boxes, Bedsteedes, Lutes, Virginals, and many things els, as I haue also said before. Some of our company which haue wandered in some places where I haue not bene, haue made certaine affirmation of 'Cyprus' which for such and other excellent vses, is also a wood of price and no small estimation.

'Maple', and also 'Wich-hazle'; wherof the inhabitants vse to make their bowes.

'Holly' a necessary thing for the making of birdlime.

'Willowes' good for the making of weares and weeles to take fish after the English manner, although the inhabitants vse only reedes, which because they are so strong as also flexible, do serue for that turne very well and sufficiently.

'Beech'and 'Ashe', good for caske, hoopes: and if neede require, plow worke, as also for many things els.

'Elme.'

'Sassafras' trees.

'Ascopo' a kinde of tree very like vnto Lawrell, the barke is hoat in tast and spicie, it is very like to that tree which Monardus describeth to bee 'Cassia Lignea' of the West Indies.

There are many other strange trees whose names I knowe not but in the 'Virginian' language, of which I am not nowe able, neither is it so conuenient for the present to trouble you with particular relatio: seeing that for timber and other necessary vses I haue named sufficient: And of many of the rest but that they may be applied to good vse, I know no cause to doubt.

Now for Stone, Bricke and Lime, thus it is. Neere vnto the Sea coast where wee dwelt, there are no kind of stones to bee found (except a fewe small pebbles about foure miles off) but such as haue bene brought from farther out of the maine. In some of our voiages wee haue seene diuers hard raggie stones, great pebbles, and a kinde of grey stone like vnto marble, of which the inhabitants make their hatchets to cleeue wood. Vpon inquirie wee heard that a little further vp into the Countrey were all sortes verie many, although of Quarries they are ignorant, neither haue they vse of any store whereupon they should haue occasion to seeke any. For if euerie housholde haue one or two to cracke Nuttes, grinde shelles, whet copper, and sometimes other stones for hatchets, they haue enough: neither vse they any digging, but onely for graues about three foote deepe: and therefore no maruaile that they know neither Quarries, nor lime stones, which both may bee in places neerer than they wot of.

In the meane time vntill there bee discouerie of sufficient store in some place or other couenient, the want of you which are and shalbe the planters therein may be as well supplied by Bricke: for the making whereof in diuers places of the countrey there is clay both excellent good, and plentie; and also by lime made of Oister shels, and of others burnt, after the maner as they vse in the Iles of Tenet and Shepy, and also in diuers other places of England: Which kinde of lime is well knowne to bee as good as any other. And of Oister shels there is plentie enough: for besides diuers other particular places where are abundance, there is one shallowe sounde along the coast, where for the space of many miles together in length, and two or three miles in breadth, the grounde is nothing els beeing but halfe a foote or a foote vnder water for the most part.

This much can I say further more of stones, that about 120. miles from our fort neere the water in the side of a hill was founde by a Gentleman of our company, a great veine of hard ragge stones, which I thought good to remember vnto you.

'Of the nature and manners of the people'

It resteth I speake a word or two of the naturall inhabitants, their natures and maners, leauing large discourse thereof vntill time more conuenient hereafter: nowe onely so farre foorth, as that you may know, how that they in respect of troubling our inhabiting and planting, are not to be feared; but that they shall haue cause both to feare and loue vs, that shall inhabite with them.

They are a people clothed with loose mantles made of Deere skins, & aprons of the same rounde about their middles; all els naked; of such as difference of statures only as wee in England; hauing no edge tooles or weapons of yron or steele to offend vs withall, neither know they how to make any: those weapos that they haue, are onlie bowes made of Witch hazle, & arrowes of reeds; flat edged truncheons also of wood about a yard long, neither haue they any thing to defend themselues but targets made of barcks; and some armours made of stickes wickered together with thread.

Their townes are but small, & neere the sea coast but few, some cotaining but 10. or 12. houses: some 20. the greatest that we haue seene haue bene but of 30. houses: if they be walled it is only done with barks of trees made fast to stakes, or els with poles onely fixed vpright and close one by another.

Their houses are made of small poles made fast at the tops in rounde forme after the maner as is vsed in many arbories in our gardens of England, in most townes couered with barkes, and in some with artificiall mattes made of long rushes; from the tops of the houses downe to the ground. The length of them is commonly double to the breadth, in some places they are but 12. and 16. yardes long, and in other some wee haue seene of foure and twentie.

In some places of the countrey one onely towne belongeth to the gouerment of a 'Wiroans' or chiefe Lorde; in other some two or three, in some sixe, eight, & more; the greatest 'Wiroans' that yet we had dealing with had but eighteene townes in his gouernmet, and able to make not aboue seuen or eight hundred fighting men at the most: The language of euery gouernment is different from any other, and the farther they are distant the greater is the difference.

Their maner of warres amongst themselues is either by sudden surprising one an other most commonly about the dawning of the day, or moone light; or els by ambushes, or some suttle deuises: Set battels are very rare, except if fall out where there are many trees, where eyther part may haue some hope of defence, after the deliuerie of euery arrow, in leaping behind some or other.

If there fall out any warres betwee vs & them; what their fight is likely to bee, we hauing aduantages against them so many maner of waies, as by our discipline, our strange weapons and deuises els; especially by ordinance great and small, it may be easily imagined; by the experience we haue had in some places, the turning vp of their heeles against vs in running away was their best defence.

In respect of vs they are a people poore, and for want of skill and iudgement in the knowledge and vse of our things, doe esteeme our trifles before thinges of greater value: Notwithstanding in their proper manner considering the want of such meanes as we haue, they seeme very ingenious; For although they haue no such tooles, nor any such craftes, sciences and artes as wee; yet in those thinges they doe, they shewe excellencie of wit. And by howe much they vpon due consideration shall finde our manner of knowledges and craftes to exceede theirs in perfection, and speed for doing or execution, by so much the more is it probable that they shoulde desire our friendships & loue, and haue the greater respect for pleasing and obeying vs. Whereby may bee hoped if meanes of good gouernment bee vsed, that they may in short time be brought to ciuilitie, and the imbracing of true religion.

Some religion they haue alreadie, which although it be farre from the truth, yet beyng as it is, there is hope it may bee the easier and sooner reformed.

They beleeue that there are many Gods which they call 'Mantoac', but of different sortes and degrees; one onely chiefe and great God, which hath bene from all eternitie. Who as they affirme when hee purposed to make the worlde, made first other goddes of a principall order to bee as meanes and instruments to bee vsed in the creation and gouernment to follow; and after the Sunne, Moone, and Starres, as pettie goddes and the instruments of the other order more principall. First they say were made waters, out of which by the gods was made all diuersitie of creatures that are visible or inuisible.

For mankind they say a woman was made first, which by the woorking of one of the goddes, conceiued and brought foorth children: And in such sort they say they had their beginning.

But how manie yeeres or ages haue passed since, they say they can make no relation, hauing no letters nor other such meanes as we to keepe recordes of the particularities of times past, but onelie tradition from father to sonne.

They thinke that all the gods are of humane shape, & therfore they represent them by images in the formes of men, which they call 'Kewasowok' one alone is called 'Kewas'; Them they place in houses appropriate or temples which they call 'Mathicomuck'; Where they woorship, praie, sing, and make manie times offerings vnto them. In some 'Machicomuck' we haue seene but on 'Kewas', in some two, and in other some three; The common sort thinke them to be also gods.

They beleeue also the immortalitie of the soule, that after this life as soone as the soule is departed from the bodie according to the workes it hath done, it is eyther carried to heaue the habitacle of gods, there to enioy perpetuall blisse and happiness, or els to a great pitte or hole, which they thinke to bee in the furthest partes of their part of the worlde towarde the sunne set, there to burne continually: the place they call 'Popogusso'.

For the confirmation of this opinion, they tolde mee two stories of two men that had been lately dead and reuiued againe, the one happened but few yeres before our comming in the countrey of a wicked man which hauing beene dead and buried, the next day the earth of the graue beeing seene to moue, was take vp againe; Who made declaration where his soule had beene, that is to saie very neere entring into 'Popogusso', had not one of the gods saued him & gaue him leaue to returne againe, and teach his friends what they should doe to auiod that terrible place of tormenr.

The other happened in the same yeere wee were there, but in a towne that was threescore miles from vs, and it was tolde mee for straunge newes that one beeing dead, buried and taken vp againe as the first, shewed that although his bodie had lien dead in the graue, yet his soule was aliue, and had trauailed farre in a long broade waie, on both sides whereof grewe most delicate and pleasaut trees, bearing more rare and excellent fruites then euer hee had seene before or was able to expresse, and at length came to most braue and faire houses, neere which hee met his father, that had beene dead before, who gaue him great charge to goe backe againe and shew his friendes what good they were to doe to enioy the pleasures of that place, which when he had done he should after come againe.

What subtilty soeuer be in the 'Wiroances' and Priestes, this opinion worketh so much in manie of the common and simple sort of people that it maketh them haue great respect to their Gouernours, and also great care what they do, to auoid torment after death, and to enjoy blisse; although nothwithstanding there is punishment ordained for malefactours, as stealers, whoremoongers, and other sortes of wicked doers; some punished with death, some with forfeitures, some with beating, according to the greatnes of the factes.

And this is the summe of their religion, which I learned by hauing special familiarity with some of their priestes. Wherein they were not so sure grounded, nor gaue such credite to their traditions and stories but through conuersing with vs they were brought into great doubts of their owne, and no small admiratio of ours, with earnest desire in many, to learne more than we had meanes for want of perfect vtterance in their language to expresse.

Most thinges they sawe with vs, as Mathematicall instruments, sea compasses, the vertue of the loadstone in drawing yron, a perspectiue glasse whereby was shewed manie strange sightes, burning glasses, wildefire woorkes, gunnes, bookes, writing and reading, spring clocks that seeme to goe of themselues, and manie other thinges that wee had, were so straunge vnto them, and so farre exceeded their capacities to comprehend the reason and meanes how they should be made and done, that they thought they were rather the works of gods then of men, or at the leastwise they had bin giuen and taught vs of the gods. Which made manie of them to haue such opinions of vs, as that if they knew not the trueth of god and religion already, it was rather to be had from vs, whom God so specially loued then from a people that were so simple, as they found themselues to be in comparison of vs. Whereupon greater credite was giuen vnto that we spake of concerning such matters.

Manie times and in euery towne where I came, according as I was able, I made declaration of the contentes of the Bible; that therein was set foorth the true and onelie GOD, and his mightie woorkes, that therein was contayned the true doctrine of saluation through Christ, which manie particularities of Miracles and chiefe poyntes of religion, as I was able then to vtter, and thought fitte for the time. And although I told them the booke materially & of itself was not of anie such vertue, as I thought they did conceiue, but onely the doctrine therein cotained; yet would many be glad to touch it, to embrace it, to kisse it, to hold it to their brests and heades, and stroke ouer all their bodie with it; to shew their hungrie desire of that knowledge which was spoken of.

The 'Wiroans' with whom we dwelt called 'Wingina', and many of his people would be glad many times to be with vs at our praiers, and many times call vpon vs both in his owne towne, as also in others whither he sometimes accompanied vs, to pray and sing Psalmes; hoping thereby to bee partaker in the same effectes which wee by that meanes also expected.

Twise this 'Wiroans' was so greiuously sicke that he was like to die, and as hee laie languishing, doubting of anie helpe by his owne priestes, and thinking he was in such daunger for offending vs and thereby our god, sent for some of vs to praie and bee a meanes to our God that it would please him either that he might liue or after death dwell with him in blisse; so likewise were the requestes of manie others in the like case.

On a time also when their corne began to wither by reason of a drouth which happened extraordinarily, fearing that it had come to passe by reason that in some thing they had displeased vs, many woulde come to vs & desire vs to praie to our God of England, that he would perserue their corne, promising that when it was ripe we also should be partakers of the fruite.

There could at no time happen any strange sicknesse, losses, hurtes, or any other crosse vnto them, but that they would impute to vs the cause or meanes therof for offending or not pleasing vs.

One other rare and strange accident, leauing others, will I mention before I ende, which mooued the whole countrey that either knew or hearde of vs, to haue vs in wonderfull admiration.

There was no towne where we had any subtile deuise practised against vs, we leauing it vnpunished or not reuenged (because wee sought by all meanes possible to win them by gentlenesse) but that within a few dayes after our departure from euerie such towne, the people began to die very fast, and many in short space; in some townes about twentie, in some fourtie, in some sixtie, & in one six score, which in trueth was very manie in respect of their numbers. This happened in no place that wee could learne but where wee had bene, where they vsed some practise against vs, and after such time; The disease also so strange, that they neither knew what it was, nor how to cure it; the like by the report of the oldest men in the countrey neuer happened before, time out of minde. A thing specially obserued by vs as also by the naturall inhabitants themselues.

Insomuch that when some of the inhabitantes which were our friends & especially the 'Wiroans Wingina' had obserued such effects in foure or fiue towns to follow their wicked practises, they were preswaded that it was the worke of our God through our meanes, and that wee by him might kil and slai whom we would without weapons and not come neere them.

And thereupon when it had happened that they had vnderstanding that any of their enemies had abused vs in our iourneyes, hearing that wee had wrought no reuenge with our weapons, & fearing vpon some cause the matter should so rest: did come and intreate vs that we woulde bee a meanes to our God that they as others that had dealt ill with vs might in like sort die; alleaging howe much it would be for our credite and profite, as also theirs; and hoping furthermore that we would do so much at their requests in respect of the friendship we professe them.

Whose entreaties although wee shewed that they were vngodlie, affirming that our God would not subiect him selfe to anie such praiers and requestes of me: that in deede all thinges haue beene and were to be done according to his good pleasure as he had ordained: ad that we to shew ourselues his true seruats ought rather to make petition for the contrarie, that they with them might liue together with vs, bee made partakers of his truth & serue him in righteousnes; but notwitstanding in such sort, that wee referre that as all other thinges, to bee done according to his diuine will & pleasure, ad as by his wisedome he had ordained to be best.

Yet because the effect fell out so sodainly and shortly after according to their desires, they thought neuertheless it came to passe by our meanes, and that we in vsing such speeches vnto them did but dissemble in the matter, and therefore came vnto vs to giue vs thankes in their manner that although wee satisfied them not in promise, yet in deedes and effect we had fulfilled their desires.

This maruelous accident in all the countrie wrought so strange opinions of vs, that some people could not tel whether to think vs gods or men, and the rather because that all the space of their sicknesse, there was no man of ours knowne to die, or that was specially sicke: they noted also that we had no women amongst vs, neither that we did care for any of theirs.

Some therefore were of opinion that wee were not borne of women, and therefore not mortall, but that wee were men of an old generation many yeeres past then risen againe to immortalitie.

Some woulde likewise seeme to prophesie that there were more of our generation yet to come, to kill theirs and take their places, as some thought the purpose was by that which was already done.

Those that were immediatly to come after vs they imagined to be in the aire, yet inuisible & without bodies, & that they by our intreaty & for the loue of vs did make the people to die in that sort as they did by shooting inuisible bullets into them.

To confirme this opinion their phisitions to excuse their ignorance in curing the disease, would not be ashemed to say, but earnestly make the simple people beleue, that the strings of blood that they sucked out of the sicke bodies, were the strings wherewithal the inuisible bullets were tied and cast.

Some also thought that we shot them ourselues out of our pieces from the place where we dwelt, and killed the people in any such towne that had offended vs as we listed, how farre distant from vs soeuer it were.

And other some saide that it was the speciall woorke of God for our sakes, as wee our selues haue cause in some sorte to thinke no lesse, whatsoeuer some doe or maie imagine to the contrarie, specially some Astrologers knowing of the Eclipse of the Sunne which wee saw the same yeere before in our voyage thytherward, which vnto them appeared very terrible. And also of a Comet which beganne to appeare but a few daies before the beginning of the said sicknesse. But to exclude them from being the speciall an accident, there are farther reasons then I thinke fit at this present to bee alleadged.

These their opinions I haue set downe the more at large that it may appeare vnto you that there is good hope they may be brought through discreet dealing and gouernement to the imbracing of the trueth, and consequently to honour, obey, feare and loue vs.

And although some of our companie towardes the ende of the yeare, shewed themselues too fierce, in slaying some of the people, in some towns, vpon causes that on our part, might easily enough haue been borne withall: yet notwithstanding because it was on their part iustly deserued, the alteration of their opinions generally & for the most part concerning vs is the lesse to bee doubted. And whatsoeuer els they may be, by carefulnesse of our selues neede nothing at all to be feared.

The best neuerthelesse in this as in all actions besides is to be endeuoured and hoped, & of the worst that may happen notice to bee taken with consideration, and as much as may be eschewed.

'The Conclusion.'

NOW I haue as I hope made relation not of so fewe and smal things but that the countrey of men that are indifferent & wel disposed maie be sufficiently liked: If there were no more knowen then I haue mentioned, which doubtlesse and in great reason is nothing to that which remaineth to bee discouered, neither the soile, nor commodities. As we haue reason so to gather by the difference we found in our trauails: for although all which I haue before spoken of, haue bin discouered & experiemented not far from the sea coast where was our abode & most of our trauailing: yet somtimes as we made our iourneies farther into the maine and countrey;

we found the soyle to bee fatter; the trees greater and to growe thinner; the grounde more firme and deeper mould; more and larger champions; finer grasse and as good as euer we saw any in England; in some places rockie and farre more high and hillie ground; more plentie of their fruites; more abondance of beastes; the more inhabited with people, and of greater pollicie & larger dominions, with greater townes and houses.

Why may wee not then looke for in good hope from the inner parts of more and greater plentie, as well of other things, as of those which wee haue alreadie discouered? Vnto the Spaniardes happened the like in discouering the maine of the West Indies. The maine also of this countrey of 'Virginia', extending some wayes so many hundreds of leagues, as otherwise then by the relation of the inhabitants wee haue most certaine knowledge of, where yet no Christian Prince hath any possession or dealing, cannot but yeeld many kinds of excellent commodities, which we in our discouerie haue not yet seene.

What hope there is els to be gathered of the nature of the climate, being answerable to the Iland of 'Iapan', the land of 'China, Persia, Jury, the Ilandes of 'Cyprus' and 'Candy', the South parts 'Greece, Italy', and 'Spaine', and of many other notable and famous countreis, because I meane not to be tedious, I leaue to your owne consideration.'

Whereby also the excellent temperature of the ayre there at all seasons, much warmer then in England, and neuer so violently hot, as sometimes is vnder & between the Tropikes, or neere them; cannot bee vnknowne vnto you without farther relation.

For the holsomnesse thereof I neede to say but thus much: that for all the want of prouision, as first of English victuall; excepting for twentie daies, wee liued only by drinking water and by the victuall of the countrey, of which some sorts were very straunge vnto vs, and might haue bene thought to haue altered our temperatures in such sort as to haue brought vs into some greeuous and dagerous diseases: secondly the wat of English meanes, for the taking of beastes, fishe, and foule, which by the helpe only of the inhabitants and their meanes, coulde not bee so suddenly and easily prouided for vs, nor in so great numbers & quantities, nor of that choise as otherwise might haue bene to our better satisfaction and contentment. Some want also wee had of clothes. Furthermore, in all our trauailes which were most speciall and often in the time of winter, our lodging was in the open aire vpon the grounde. And yet I say for all this, there were but foure of our whole company (being one hundred and eight) that died all the yeere and that but at the latter ende thereof and vpon none of the aforesaide causes. For all foure especially three were feeble, weake, and sickly persons before euer they came thither, and those that knewe them much marueyled that they liued so long beeing in that case, or had aduentured to trauaile.

Seing therefore the ayre there is so temperate and holsome, the soyle so fertile and yeelding such commodities as I haue before mentioned, the voyage also thither to and fro beeing sufficiently experimented, to bee perfourmed thrise a yeere with ease and at any season thereof: And the dealing of 'Sir Walter Raleigh' so liberall in large giuing and grauting lande there, as is alreadie knowen, with many helpes and furtherances els: (The least that hee hath graunted hath beene fiue hundred acres to a man onely for the aduenture of his person): I hope there reamine no cause whereby the action should be misliked.

If that those which shall thither trauaile to inhabite and plant bee but reasonably prouided for the first yere as those are which were transported the last, and beeing there doe vse but that diligence and care as is requisite, and as they may with eese: There is no doubt but for the time following they may haue victuals that is excellent good and plentie enough; some more Englishe sortes of cattaile also hereafter, as some haue bene before, and are there yet remaining, may and shall bee God willing thiter transported: So likewise our kinde of fruites, rootes, and hearbes may bee there planted and sowed, as some haue bene alreadie, and proue wel: And in short time also they may raise of those sortes of commodities which I haue spoken of as shall both enrich theselues, as also others that shall deale with them.

And this is all the fruites of our labours, that I haue thought necessary to aduertise you of at this present: what els concerneth the nature and manners of the inhabitants of 'Virginia': The number with the particularities of the voyages thither made; and of the actions of such that haue bene by 'Sir Walter Raleigh' therein and there imployed, many worthy to bee remembered; as of the first discouerers of the Countrey: of our generall for the time 'Sir Richard Greinuile'; and after his departure, of our Gouernour there Master 'Rafe Lane'; with diuers other directed and imployed vnder theyr gouernement: Of the Captaynes and Masters of the voyages

made since for transporation; of the Gouernour and assistants of those alredie transported, as of many persons, accidets, and thinges els, I haue ready in a discourse by
it selfe in maner of a Chronicle according to the course of times, and when time
shall bee thought conuenient shall be also published.

This referring my relation to your fauourable constructions, expecting good
successe of the action, from him which is to be acknowledged the authour and
gouernour not only of this but of all things els, I take my leaue of you, this moneth
of Februarii, 1588.

F I N I S.

The Codes Of Hammurabi And Moses
W. W. Davies

QTY

The discovery of the Hammurabi Code is one of the greatest achievements of archaeology, and is of paramount interest, not only to the student of the Bible, but also to all those interested in ancient history...

Religion ISBN: *1-59462-338-4*   **Pages:132**
MSRP $12.95

The Theory of Moral Sentiments
Adam Smith

QTY

This work from 1749. contains original theories of conscience amd moral judgment and it is the foundation for systemof morals.

Philosophy ISBN: *1-59462-777-0*   **Pages:536**
MSRP $19.95

Jessica's First Prayer
Hesba Stretton

QTY

In a screened and secluded corner of one of the many railway-bridges which span the streets of London there could be seen a few years ago, from five o'clock every morning until half past eight, a tidily set-out coffee-stall, consisting of a trestle and board, upon which stood two large tin cans, with a small fire of charcoal burning under each so as to keep the coffee boiling during the early hours of the morning when the work-people were thronging into the city on their way to their daily toil...

Pages:84

Childrens ISBN: *1-59462-373-2*   *MSRP $9.95*

My Life and Work
Henry Ford

QTY

Henry Ford revolutionized the world with his implementation of mass production for the Model T automobile. Gain valuable business insight into his life and work with his own auto-biography... "We have only started on our development of our country we have not as yet, with all our talk of wonderful progress, done more than scratch the surface. The progress has been wonderful enough but..."

Pages:300

Biographies/ ISBN: *1-59462-198-5*   *MSRP $21.95*

The Art of Cross-Examination
Francis Wellman

QTY

I presume it is the experience of every author, after his first book is published upon an important subject, to be almost overwhelmed with a wealth of ideas and illustrations which could readily have been included in his book, and which to his own mind, at least, seem to make a second edition inevitable. Such certainly was the case with me; and when the first edition had reached its sixth impression in five months, I rejoiced to learn that it seemed to my publishers that the book had met with a sufficiently favorable reception to justify a second and considerably enlarged edition. ..

Reference   **ISBN:** *1-59462-647-2*

Pages:412
MSRP $19.95

On the Duty of Civil Disobedience
Henry David Thoreau

QTY

Thoreau wrote his famous essay, On the Duty of Civil Disobedience, as a protest against an unjust but popular war and the immoral but popular institution of slave-owning. He did more than write—he declined to pay his taxes, and was hauled off to gaol in consequence. Who can say how much this refusal of his hastened the end of the war and of slavery ?

Law   **ISBN:** *1-59462-747-9*

Pages:48
MSRP $7.45

Dream Psychology Psychoanalysis for Beginners
Sigmund Freud

QTY

Sigmund Freud, born Sigismund Schlomo Freud (May 6, 1856 - September 23, 1939), was a Jewish-Austrian neurologist and psychiatrist who co-founded the psychoanalytic school of psychology. Freud is best known for his theories of the unconscious mind, especially involving the mechanism of repression; his redefinition of sexual desire as mobile and directed towards a wide variety of objects; and his therapeutic techniques, especially his understanding of transference in the therapeutic relationship and the presumed value of dreams as sources of insight into unconscious desires.

Psychology   **ISBN:** *1-59462-905-6*

Pages:196
MSRP $15.45

The Miracle of Right Thought
Orison Swett Marden

QTY

Believe with all of your heart that you will do what you were made to do. When the mind has once formed the habit of holding cheerful, happy, prosperous pictures, it will not be easy to form the opposite habit. It does not matter how improbable or how far away this realization may see, or how dark the prospects may be, if we visualize them as best we can, as vividly as possible, hold tenaciously to them and vigorously struggle to attain them, they will gradually become actualized, realized in the life. But a desire, a longing without endeavor, a yearning abandoned or held indifferently will vanish without realization.

Self Help   **ISBN:** *1-59462-644-8*

Pages:360
MSRP $25.45

QTY

The Rosicrucian Cosmo-Conception Mystic Christianity by *Max Heindel*   ISBN: *1-59462-188-8*   **$38.95**
The Rosicrucian Cosmo-conception is not dogmatic, neither does it appeal to any other authority than the reason of the student. It is: not controversial, but is: sent forth in the, hope that it may help to clear.
New Age/Religion Pages 646

Abandonment To Divine Providence by *Jean-Pierre de Caussade*   ISBN: *1-59462-228-0*   **$25.95**
"The Rev. Jean Pierre de Caussade was one of the most remarkable spiritual writers of the Society of Jesus in France in the 18th Century. His death took place at Toulouse in 1751. His works have gone through many editions and have been republished...
Inspirational/Religion Pages 400

Mental Chemistry by *Charles Haanel*   ISBN: *1-59462-192-6*   **$23.95**
Mental Chemistry allows the change of material conditions by combining and appropriately utilizing the power of the mind. Much like applied chemistry creates something new and unique out of careful combinations of chemicals the mastery of mental chemistry...
New Age Pages 354

The Letters of Robert Browning and Elizabeth Barret Barrett 1845-1846 vol II   ISBN: *1-59462-193-4*   **$35.95**
by *Robert Browning and Elizabeth Barrett*
Biographies Pages 596

Gleanings In Genesis (volume I) by *Arthur W. Pink*   ISBN: *1-59462-130-6*   **$27.45**
Appropriately has Genesis been termed "the seed plot of the Bible" for in it we have, in germ form, almost all of the great doctrines which are afterwards fully developed in the books of Scripture which follow...
Religion/Inspirational Pages 420

The Master Key by *L. W. de Laurence*   ISBN: *1-59462-001-6*   **$30.95**
In no branch of human knowledge has there been a more lively increase of the spirit of research during the past few years than in the study of Psychology, Concentration and Mental Discipline. The requests for authentic lessons in Thought Control, Mental Discipline and...   *New Age/Business Pages 422*

The Lesser Key Of Solomon Goetia by *L. W. de Laurence*   ISBN: *1-59462-092-X*   **$9.95**
This translation of the first book of the "Lernegton" which is now for the first time made accessible to students of Talismanic Magic was done, after careful collation and edition, from numerous Ancient Manuscripts in Hebrew, Latin, and French...
New Age/Occult Pages 92

Rubaiyat Of Omar Khayyam by *Edward Fitzgerald*   ISBN:*1-59462-332-5*   **$13.95**
Edward Fitzgerald, whom the world has already learned, in spite of his own efforts to remain within the shadow of anonymity, to look upon as one of the rarest poets of the century, was born at Bredfield, in Suffolk, on the 31st of March, 1809. He was the third son of John Purcell...   *Music Pages 172*

Ancient Law by *Henry Maine*   ISBN: *1-59462-128-4*   **$29.95**
The chief object of the following pages is to indicate some of the earliest ideas of mankind, as they are reflected in Ancient Law, and to point out the relation of those ideas to modern thought.
Religion/History Pages 452

Far-Away Stories by *William J. Locke*   ISBN: *1-59462-129-2*   **$19.45**
"Good wine needs no bush, but a collection of mixed vintages does. And this book is just such a collection. Some of the stories I do not want to remain buried for ever in the museum files of dead magazine-numbers an author's not unpardonable vanity..."   *Fiction Pages 272*

Life of David Crockett by *David Crockett*   ISBN: *1-59462-250-7*   **$27.45**
"Colonel David Crockett was one of the most remarkable men of the times in which he lived. Born in humble life, but gifted with a strong will, an indomitable courage, and unremitting perseverance...
Biographies/New Age Pages 424

Lip-Reading by *Edward Nitchie*   ISBN: *1-59462-206-X*   **$25.95**
Edward B. Nitchie, founder of the New York School for the Hard of Hearing, now the Nitchie School of Lip-Reading, Inc, wrote "LIP-READING Principles and Practice". The development and perfecting of this meritorious work on lip-reading was an undertaking...   *How-to Pages 400*

A Handbook of Suggestive Therapeutics, Applied Hypnotism, Psychic Science   ISBN: *1-59462-214-0*   **$24.95**
by *Henry Munro*
Health/New Age/Health/Self-help Pages 376

A Doll's House: and Two Other Plays by *Henrik Ibsen*   ISBN: *1-59462-112-8*   **$19.95**
Henrik Ibsen created this classic when in revolutionary 1848 Rome. Introducing some striking concepts in playwriting for the realist genre, this play has been studied the world over.
Fiction/Classics/Plays 308

The Light of Asia by *sir Edwin Arnold*   ISBN: *1-59462-204-3*   **$13.95**
In this poetic masterpiece, Edwin Arnold describes the life and teachings of Buddha. The man who was to become known as Buddha to the world was born as Prince Gautama of India but he rejected the worldly riches and abandoned the reigns of power when... Religion/History/Biographies Pages 170

The Complete Works of Guy de Maupassant by *Guy de Maupassant*   ISBN: *1-59462-157-8*   **$16.95**
"For days and days, nights and nights, I had dreamed of that first kiss which was to consecrate our engagement, and I knew not on what spot I should put my lips..."   *Fiction/Classics Pages 240*

The Art of Cross-Examination by *Francis L. Wellman*   ISBN: *1-59462-309-0*   **$26.95**
Written by a renowned trial lawyer, Wellman imparts his experience and uses case studies to explain how to use psychology to extract desired information through questioning.
How-to/Science/Reference Pages 408

Answered or Unanswered? by *Louisa Vaughan*   ISBN: *1-59462-248-5*   **$10.95**
Miracles of Faith in China
Religion Pages 112

The Edinburgh Lectures on Mental Science (1909) by *Thomas*   ISBN: *1-59462-008-3*   **$11.95**
This book contains the substance of a course of lectures recently given by the writer in the Queen Street Hall, Edinburgh. Its purpose is to indicate the Natural Principles governing the relation between Mental Action and Material Conditions...   *New Age/Psychology Pages 148*

Ayesha by *H. Rider Haggard*   ISBN: *1-59462-301-5*   **$24.95**
Verily and indeed it is the unexpected that happens! Probably if there was one person upon the earth from whom the Editor of this, and of a certain previous history, did not expect to hear again...
Classics Pages 380

Ayala's Angel by *Anthony Trollope*   ISBN: *1-59462-352-X*   **$29.95**
The two girls were both pretty, but Lucy who was twenty-one who supposed to be simple and comparatively unattractive, whereas Ayala was credited, as her Bombwhat romantic name might show, with poetic charm and a taste for romance. Ayala when her father died was nineteen... Fiction Pages 484

The American Commonwealth by *James Bryce*   ISBN: *1-59462-286-8*   **$34.45**
An interpretation of American democratic political theory. It examines political mechanics and society from the perspective of Scotsman James Bryce
Politics Pages 572

Stories of the Pilgrims by *Margaret P. Pumphrey*   ISBN: *1-59462-116-0*   **$17.95**
This book explores pilgrims religious oppression in England as well as their escape to Holland and eventual crossing to America on the Mayflower, and their early days in New England...
History Pages 268

QTY

The Fasting Cure *by Sinclair Upton*   ISBN: *1-59462-222-1* **$13.95**

In the Cosmopolitan Magazine for May, 1910, and in the Contemporary Review (London) for April, 1910, I published an article dealing with my experiences in fasting. I have written a great many magazine articles, but never one which attracted so much attention... New Age/Self Help/Health Pages 164

Hebrew Astrology *by Sepharial*   ISBN: *1-59462-308-2* **$13.45**

In these days of advanced thinking it is a matter of common observation that we have left many of the old landmarks behind and that we are now pressing forward to greater heights and to a wider horizon than that which represented the mind-content of our progenitors... Astrology Pages 144

Thought Vibration or The Law of Attraction in the Thought World   ISBN: *1-59462-127-6* **$12.95**

by William Walker Atkinson   Psychology/Religion Pages 144

Optimism *by Helen Keller*   ISBN: *1-59462-108-X* **$15.95**

Helen Keller was blind, deaf, and mute since 19 months old, yet famously learned how to overcome these handicaps, communicate with the world, and spread her lectures promoting optimism. An inspiring read for everyone... Biographies/Inspirational Pages 84

Sara Crewe *by Frances Burnett*   ISBN: *1-59462-360-0* **$9.45**

In the first place, Miss Minchin lived in London. Her home was a large, dull, tall one, in a large, dull square, where all the houses were alike, and all the sparrows were alike, and where all the door-knockers made the same heavy sound... Childrens/Classic Pages 85

The Autobiography of Benjamin Franklin *by Benjamin Franklin*   ISBN: *1-59462-135-7* **$24.95**

The Autobiography of Benjamin Franklin has probably been more extensively read than any other American historical work, and no other book of its kind has had such ups and downs of fortune. Franklin lived for many years in England, where he was agent... Biographies/History Pages 332

Name	
Email	
Telephone	
Address	
City, State ZIP	

☐ **Credit Card**   ☐ **Check / Money Order**

Credit Card Number	
Expiration Date	
Signature	

Please Mail to: Book Jungle
PO Box 2226
Champaign, IL 61825
or Fax to: 630-214-0564

ORDERING INFORMATION

web: *www.bookjungle.com*
email: *sales@bookjungle.com*
fax: *630-214-0564*
mail: *Book Jungle PO Box 2226 Champaign, IL 61825*
or PayPal *to sales@bookjungle.com*

Please contact us for bulk discounts

DIRECT-ORDER TERMS

**20% Discount if You Order
Two or More Books**
Free Domestic Shipping!
Accepted: Master Card, Visa,
Discover, American Express

www.ingramcontent.com/pod-product-compliance
Lightning Source LLC
Chambersburg PA
CBHW081202170626
46813CB00009B/3296